HELPING CHILDREN
DEAL WITH
CONFLICT

Jenny Mosley and Helen Sonnet

Permission to photocopy

This book contains materials which may be reproduced by photocopier or other means for use by the purchaser. The permission is granted on the understanding that these copies will be used within the educational establishment of the purchaser. The book and all its contents remain copyright. Copies may be made without reference to the publisher or the licensing scheme for the making of photocopies operated by the Publishers' Licensing Agency.

Acknowledgements

This is the third book we have produced with LDA in the Helping Children Deal with … series. Corin has been our editor for all three books and many others too. He is extraordinarily calm and wise. When we are tense and fail to put our theories into practice, he is always there to calm us quietly. Thank you, Corin, for sharing your skills and talents. LDA is a wonderful company to work with. We have particularly valued the support and expertise of Cathy Griffin and Debbie Risley on this and other projects.

The rights of Jenny Mosley and Helen Sonnet to be identified as the authors of this work have been asserted by them in accordance with sections 77 and 78 of the Copyright, Designs and Patents Act 1988.

MT10015
ISBN-13: 978 1 85503 412 9
© Jenny Mosley and Helen Sonnet
Illustrations © Jane Eccles
All rights reserved
First published 2007

Printed in the UK for LDA
Abbeygate House, East Road, Cambridge, CB1 1DB, UK

CONTENTS

Introduction 4

Conducting Circle Time 5

What does falling out mean? 6

People have different views 8

Dealing with differences 9

Encouraging co-operation 11

A co-operative task 12

Causes of conflict 15

Looking at situations 16

Looking at what people do when they fall out 18

Making up is hard to do 19

Looking at arguments 21

Aggressive, passive and assertive 24

The skills of negotiation 27

Looking at wrong assumptions 29

The peace process 31

Using 'I' statements 34

Looking at the importance of listening 35

Helping and hindering the peace process 38

Using the creative arts to explore conflict resolution 40

Helping children who are unable to resolve conflict 42

Resources 47

INTRODUCTION

As you return to your classroom, you are told that an argument involving your children occurred at playtime. They are still bickering. You know from experience that it will take at least 20 minutes for them to calm down.

Two children have fallen out over something one of them said. Both children are in tears and valuable time is needed to help to resolve their quarrel.

Are these scenarios familiar? How much time do you spend each week helping to sort out disputes and friendship problems? It's probably far more than you can afford. Dealing with enraged or upset children can be time consuming and stressful.

Wouldn't it be wonderful if children were skilful enough to sort out their disputes in a reasonable and independent manner?

This book is intended for headteachers, teachers, teaching assistants, learning mentors – in fact, anyone who helps children learn how to resolve conflict issues. It contains an invaluable programme of activities for this area, one which can be incorporated into your Circle Times or delivered as part of your provision for SEAL (Social and Emotional Aspects of Learning) and PSHE. The programme complements the 'Getting On and Falling Out' theme of the SEAL materials.

This book explains conflict resolution in simple, meaningful terms, teaching children the skills needed to resolve conflicts independently. By the end of the programme, children should be able to make the following statements:

- I understand what conflict is and why it occurs.
- I know how to recognise feelings of anger and a desire to retaliate.
- I know how to negotiate.
- I know how to manage negative emotions.
- I understand that people have different views and needs that can be respected through listening, understanding and negotiation.

Through a variety of games and activities your children are given opportunities to learn, consider and practise the important skills necessary for conflict resolution. These enjoyable activities and games are designed to promote thoughtfulness, self-awareness and co-operation.

You are shown how to set up a successful peace process for children to use to resolve differences, including tips on what does and doesn't work and useful photocopiable resources. The book also includes a section to help you deal with children who are frequently involved in disputes or who lack the opportunity to develop their social skills at home.

By teaching children conflict-resolution skills not only will you be reducing the amount of time you have to spend sorting out quarrels, but you will also be equipping them with valuable skills for life.

Each session in the programme is designed to build on the one before it. This should help children develop their understanding and skills systematically. However, if you do not want to run an in-depth programme or if you have a specific need, you can select the activities and sections that you feel are of particular relevance to your children's needs.

CONDUCTING CIRCLE TIME

To lead the Circle Time sessions successfully, you need to understand the stages of a Circle Time as part of the Quality Circle Time model.

Meeting up – playing a game

Always aim to begin a Circle Time with a warm-up activity. This helps everyone to relax. It is useful for the game to involve the children changing places as this opens up the opportunity for new friendships and stronger group dynamics.

Warming up – breaking the silence

In a Circle Time, everyone has the right to speak and the responsibility to listen. This stage should be a round using a sentence stem such as 'My favourite sport is . . .'. The leader introduces this, it goes all the way round the circle until it gets back to them, and then they complete the stem.

A small speaking object, such as a painted wooden egg or a small soft toy, is held by the person who is speaking. They have the right to speak without interruption. The object is passed to the next person once the holder has spoken. Any child who does not wish to speak may say 'Pass' when the object is handed to them.

Some children may pass because they are unsure of what to say or are being uncooperative. Try to tell your group what the round is going to be about the day before the Circle Time so that they have a chance to prepare. They can write their sentence down if necessary.

If you work with young children, holding a number of smaller circles beforehand can be useful. You can use a puppet to explain the forthcoming Circle Time. A child can tell the puppet their sentence. If needed, the puppet can speak for them in the bigger circle.

Opening up – exploring issues

This is the most challenging stage as it is when issues are explored in an open forum. This can include discussion, role play, creative activities and puppets. This is the time when new skills can be learnt, new insights reached and plans agreed.

Cheering up – celebrating the positive

This stage affirms the work of the open forum. It should be a positive time that could be used as a way to highlight the effective use of the strategies learnt as part of the conflict programme.

Calming down – bringing children forward

Using a ritual to close a Circle Time makes the transition to the next activity as calm as possible. This can be done by playing a quiet game, listening to relaxing music or using a visualisation. This gives space and time for the learning of the open forum to sink in.

These five stages are the foundations of Quality Circle Time. For the Circle Times in this book we have focused on the opening-up stage to show how it can be used to explore conflict resolution.

WHAT DOES FALLING OUT MEAN?

This introduction to the programme looks at the reasons why people sometimes fall out with one another.

Learning goal

I know that feelings, thoughts and behaviour are linked.

Resources

A beanbag, a flipchart and a pen

What to do

Opening activity

Start the session with the circle game Afloat in a Boat. Ask the children to sit in a circle and teach them the following chant:

Thirty [or however many are in your group] *children*
Were floating in a boat.
There was a loud shout
And one fell out.

As you begin the chant, pass the beanbag to the child on your left. The children continue to pass the beanbag until the chant ends. Whoever is holding the beanbag at this point must move to the centre of the circle. The chant resumes with the child on the left of the one who has moved.

Play more rounds like this, depending on how much time you have. Before the chant begins again, the child/children in the centre are allowed to guess who they think will be out this time. If they are correct, they are allowed to rejoin the circle. Don't forget to adjust the number used in the rhyme each time.

Going deeper

Remind the group that they have been playing an enjoyable game about people falling out of a boat. Ask them to suggest other meanings for the words **falling out**. Make a list of their responses in the middle of the flipchart. They might include quarrelling, squabbling, breaking friends, having an argument, and so on. Draw a line round this list.

Ask the children to sit quietly and think about a time when they had a falling-out with someone. This might have happened at school, at home or in the park. Reassure them that you won't be asking them to tell anyone about this incident. Now, ask them to think about how the falling-out made them feel. They can think about how it made them feel when it was happening, immediately afterwards or when they had to see that person or those people again. Ask each child to think of a word to describe how they felt. Go round the group and ask each child to contribute the word they thought of. A sentence stem might help with this; for example: 'When I had a falling-out I felt …'. Write the suggested words around the circled words on the flipchart.

If you have children who are reluctant to think of a personal experience of conflict, for whatever reason, ask them to think of an incident from a story or film and reflect on how the participants may have felt.

Time to reflect

Ask the children if the words they have just provided describe pleasant or uncomfortable feelings. Do these words describe feelings that they would want to have or that they would rather avoid?

Read out the list of words that you circled and point out that when these things happen we often end up feeling like the words outside the circle. Explain that a word that joins these words together is **conflict** and that you will all be spending the next few weeks looking at ways to reduce the amount of conflict that happens and to make up if a conflict does occur.

Closing activity

Ask the children to lie on their backs where they are sitting in the circle with their heads towards the middle. If space is tight, ask them to sit quietly with their hands in their laps, their eyes closed and their shoulders relaxed. Tell the children that you are going to describe an imaginary journey. Use the following script:

Imagine that it is a beautiful sunny day. You are lying on the deck of a boat that is gently bobbing up and down on a clear blue sea. You can feel a warm breeze on your face … You drift towards some land. As you do, you can hear the sound of the waves breaking on a beach, people playing games, sea birds calling … You float towards a jetty where your boat comes to rest gently. We're going to come back to the classroom now. I want you to stretch your arms slowly and carefully. Rotate your wrist joints. Stretch your legs and rotate your ankle joints. Open your eyes and smile at the people nearby.

> **Action plan**
>
> Creative visualisations are a useful means to calm children who are angry, anxious or worried. They work well to bring a discussion to an end when an issue has been explored or emotions have run high. Try to develop the use of these as part of your teaching.

Extension activity

Ask each child in your group to choose a feeling from the list made earlier. They could look up their word in a dictionary and write out the definition(s). They could also use a thesaurus to find other words that have a similar meaning. These findings could be made into a wall display. Alternatively, you could give each child a piece of paper. Ask them to write their chosen word in the centre and then explore its meaning using colours and lines – spiky and red might be angry, scratchy and dark might be irritable.

PEOPLE HAVE DIFFERENT VIEWS

In this session, the children consider that many subjects can generate a range of views and feelings.

Learning goal

I know that people have feelings and understand that they might experience and show these feelings differently depending on the circumstances.

Resources

A long skipping rope or a piece of chalk

What to do

Opening activity

Create a long line on the floor by laying out the rope or drawing a chalk line. Tell the children that you are going to read a statement. Each child needs to decide how strongly they feel about the statement. Once you have read a statement from the list that follows, ask for volunteers to stand on the line in a place that reflects how they feel about it. If they strongly agree they stand at one end of the line. If they strongly disagree, they stand at the other end. If their view lies somewhere between, they stand on the line at a point that corresponds to the intensity of their feeling. Here are some statements to get you started:

- I like hot custard.
- A tidy room is important.
- Football is the most exciting sport.
- Film stars get paid too much money.
- A dog makes the best pet.
- Camping is the best sort of holiday.

You might like to ask children to explain why they chose to stand where they did on the line.

Going deeper

At the end of this activity, ask the children what they noticed about what happened. Someone is likely to say that not everyone stood in the same place. This will help you to highlight the range of views that exist in a group. Point out that sometimes the views expressed in the activity were very strong, with children standing at either end of the line. However, the same children did not always hold extreme views on each statement. On some matters they stood in the middle. Discuss how the number in favour or opposed to a view varied from statement to statement.

This activity is a good way to discuss the fact that just as people are physically different, they are also different in their views and opinions.

Time to reflect

Remind the children that the purpose of this programme is to help them deal with conflict effectively. Explain that one of the reasons for disagreements is that we are all different, as they saw in the earlier activity. There might be fewer arguments if we agreed about everything, but life would be boring if it were the case. Explain that our differences are what make us interesting individuals. We have to allow each other to be different. This involves understanding that we won't always agree with everyone.

Explain that there is a rule to help us to do this. It is 'We are kind and helpful; we don't hurt other people's feelings.' This rule means that we understand that other people may like things that we don't and may have opinions that we don't agree with. Despite these differences, it is possible to find ways to live together without their causing problems. The rule also means that we are not allowed to be different in ways that hurt other people. So, it is fine to hate hot custard but it is not fine to prevent others from eating it. There is a word to describe this way of getting along with other people; it is **tolerance**.

Closing activity

End the session with a circle game. Call out a description such as 'Everyone who has a cat'. Everyone who fits into this category must stand up and swap places with someone else who stood up. Repeat this with different descriptions so that everyone has a chance to move around.

> ### Action plan
> Use opportunities in maths to explore differences through data collection and analysis. These can be very flexible tools and can be used to explore views on issues as well as personal differences.

Extension activity

Put the children into groups of four. Give each child a sheet of paper and a pencil. Ask them to fold the paper into quarters and draw a simple shape or picture in one quarter. They need to do this quickly. Call 'Change' after about 30 seconds. Each child then passes their sheet of paper to another member of their group. This child must copy the first picture in one of the three empty quarters, changing it slightly from the original – in size, shape or orientation. Repeat the process twice more. Use the completed sheets to make a display entitled 'Same but different'.

DEALING WITH DIFFERENCES

This session helps children to develop tolerance for everyone's right to their own views and feelings.

Learning goal

I value and respect the thoughts, feelings, beliefs and values of other people.

Resources

None

What to do

Opening activity

To lead this game you need to stand in front of the group and perform an action such as clapping your hands. If you say 'Same', the children copy you. If you perform an action and say 'Different', the children perform another action of their choice. Those who fail to follow the instructions correctly must leave the group.

You could play until you have a winner or for a specified time.

Going deeper

Put the children in pairs. Tell them that one child in each pair must agree with a statement that you are going to say and the other child must disagree. Each child needs to think of reasons for their position. Read the statements that follow one at a time and allow time between them for the pairs to explore their different viewpoints:

- Hamsters are better pets than cats.
- Children shouldn't eat sweets.
- Parents should do what their children tell them.

For the next three statements, tell the pairs that they both need to agree with the statements, exploring reasons why:

- Watching television is bad for you.
- School uniform is a good thing.
- It's good for children to have homework.

Call the children into a circle. Ask them in what way their conversations felt different when they had to disagree in their pairs compared to when they agreed.

Time to reflect

Discuss with the children how they felt when the other person in their pair disagreed with them. Were they tempted to try to change the other person's view? You could explore how we should not be closed to reassessing our own views but should not feel forced by someone else to change them. Remind them that everyone has a right to their own views.

Closing activity

End the session with a circle game that explores different views. Call out a statement such as 'Cereal is the best breakfast food.' Everyone who agrees with the statement must stand up and swap places with someone else who stood up. Repeat this with different statements so that everyone has a chance to move around.

Action plan

Develop the use of balanced discussion to explore school issues such as uniform or playing football in the playground. Announce the issue beforehand, gather arguments for and against, ask volunteers to sum up the points, and hold a vote to see which view was held by most. The results of such debates could be used to increase your pupils' involvement in school decisions.

Extension activity

Read a story or poem that has more than one character to the children. Ask them to rewrite or retell it from the point of view of one of the characters. For instance, they could tell 'Sleeping Beauty' from the point of view of the prince or one of the fairy godmothers.

ENCOURAGING CO-OPERATION

This session looks at ways to get on with others when working in a group.

Learning goal

I know what helps a group work together well.

Resources

A flipchart and a pen. Postcards or pictures cut into six pieces, enough for each child to have a piece.

What to do

Opening activity

Ask the children to spread out and walk around the work area. When you say 'Stop', they must turn to the nearest person and take it in turns to tell each other, for example, what their favourite television programme is. Repeat this several times, changing the subject for each round and encouraging the children to choose a different partner each time. In some of the later rounds, ask the children to make groups of three or four.

Going deeper

Shuffle the pieces of postcard and give one to each child. If any child has to sit out, make sure they join in this game on another occasion. Tell the children that they need to find the other children who have pieces of the same picture. Give the children a couple of minutes to do this, depending on the size of your group. Once a group of six is complete, they sit down and assemble their picture.

Give each group of six a category to discuss. Although they may have a number of views within their group, they must agree on one choice without exerting pressure on anyone. Explain that each item doesn't have to be their favourite, but it does have to be something that they all agree on, which may involve some compromise. Try the following categories to get them started:

- a cartoon character;
- a hobby;
- a chocolate bar;
- a colour;
- a book.

Tell the children that you will be looking for groups who are co-operating well. Make sure that you feed back on what you see while the activity is going on, highlighting what is positive and a good model of working.

Time to reflect

After the activity, ask each small group what they decided on for each of the categories, or as many as they had time to complete. Draw the children's attention to how the groups' choices were different at times. Discuss how easy or difficult they found the task. Explore the successful strategies they used to come to decisions and how they solved any problems they encountered. Make a list on the flipchart of the helpful strategies they suggest and the ones that you observed. These might include:

- listening carefully;
- waiting for a turn to speak;
- using a quiet voice;
- checking that everyone is agreed;
- including everyone;
- repeating what they think is agreed.

Ask the children to suggest other times when they might find these strategies useful, such as during other lessons, in the playground or in the lunch hall.

Closing activity

Put the children into groups of four or five. Ask each small group to find a space and make the outline of a number on the floor using some or all of their group members. Repeat this a few times, changing each group's number every time. Use the opportunity to commend children using skills mentioned in the previous parts of this session.

> **Action plan**
>
> Make sure that you reinforce positive behaviour by drawing attention to it specifically. Focus on productive groupwork behaviours by praising them as follows: 'Well done, [name], you are using very good listening skills today' or 'Very good, [name], you are taking turns well.' Ask the children to nominate others in their group for particularly helpful behaviour.

Extension activity

Put the children into groups and give each a range of different materials and equipment, such as a sheet of paper, a pair of scissors, a box of paperclips, a yoghurt pot, some sticky tape, and so on. Tell the groups that you want them to work together to create something interesting to show the others but don't specify what. Allow 20 to 30 minutes for the activity. Watch them as they work and make a note of any good co-operation and social skills.

When the time is up, call the children together and ask each group to present their creation. Make comments about the helpful ways in which each group worked together and how they tackled the challenges they faced. Make a display of the creations with the comments on good co-operation beside them.

A CO-OPERATIVE TASK

In this session, the children explore strategies for group cohesion.

Learning goal

I can tell you what helps a group work well together.

Resources

The matching pictures or postcard sets from the previous session, a copy of the table on page 14 and a pencil for each group.

What to do

Opening activity

Use the cut-up postcards or pictures from the previous session (see page 11) to sort the children into mixed-ability groups of about six. Adjust the size of the groups to include all the children. Explain that you are going to give them a task to complete, during which you want them to work as a team. Tell them that an alien is coming to stay with them for one day. They need to plan the day's events and meals to show the alien how children live. They must try to make the day representative of the views of everyone in their group by discussion and compromise. Allow the children about 15 to 20 minutes for this task.

HELPING CHILDREN DEAL WITH CONFLICT

Closing activity

Explain that you will call out a number. Each group is to work out how to make this number by putting their feet, heads or hands on the floor. They are not allowed to use chairs. For example, if you call out 'Eight', some children may have to stand on one foot.

> **Action plan**
>
> Use the information from the sessions to make a group charter to establish good teamwork rules for activities, such as 'We listen to each other', 'We take turns to speak.' You could make a poster to display these rules.

Extension activity

Many group activities – such as playground games, dominoes, Pass the Parcel – have rules to ensure that everyone behaves fairly. Ask each group to choose a game or activity and to write out the main rules, giving reasons for their use.

Going deeper

Ask a volunteer from each group to explain their plan for the day to the other children. After the presentations, discuss what made the task easy or difficult to complete. As part of this process, ask each group to complete the table on page 14 together by ticking the appropriate boxes. A tick in the column showing a sun means they did the task well, a tick in the column with a sun and cloud means there is room for improvement and a tick in the column with a cloud means they did not work well together.

Time to reflect

Look at each completed table and ask the children to suggest ways in which each group could improve their performance, such as:

> - appoint a group chairperson to manage the proceedings and encourage all members to contribute;
> - give each member the same number of counters and ask them to hand one in each time they speak;
> - use a sand timer or counter to limit the time each child speaks.

A co-operative task

	☀	⛅	☁
We all had a turn to speak.			
We listened to each other.			
We agreed on each item.			
We resolved any disagreements.			

A co-operative task

	☀	⛅	☁
We all had a turn to speak.			
We listened to each other.			
We agreed on each item.			
We resolved any disagreements.			

A co-operative task

	☀	⛅	☁
We all had a turn to speak.			
We listened to each other.			
We agreed on each item.			
We resolved any disagreements.			

© *Helping Children Deal with Conflict* LDA   Permission to Photocopy

CAUSES OF CONFLICT

In this session, the children consider causes of conflict.

Learning goal
I know that my actions affect other people and can have an impact on how they feel.

Resources
Puppets or play figures

What to do

Opening activity
Ask the children to put on a different expression that shows how they might feel in each of the following situations:

- You are opening a birthday present.
- You have fallen over and hurt your knee.
- You hear a strange noise at night.
- Your best friend has just arrived to play with you.
- Someone has got a new bike and you have wanted one for a long time.
- Someone has called you an unkind name.

If you think that the children might find this activity difficult, you can use the expressions fans in the resources section of the SEAL pack.

Going deeper
Ask the children how they would feel in the last situation – probably angry or sad. Remind the children how they had talked previously about falling out because of different people's views and needs. Explain that in this session they are going to look at some of the other reasons why people fall out.

Ask the children why they sometimes fall out with their friends. They are likely to mention reasons such as:

- wanting to do different things;
- wanting to use the same toy;
- going off with another child;
- a dispute over a game.

Ask the children why people fall out with people they like. Discuss some of the reasons why we may fall out with even our closest friends.

Divide the children up into small groups and give them some puppets or play figures. Ask each group to create a short drama in which their characters fall out. Stress that you want to see only the events that lead up to the point of falling out. Give them 10 to 15 minutes to prepare their dramas, and then ask each group in turn to perform their work.

Time to reflect
After the dramas, ask the children to think about strategies that could have helped the characters in each scene to avoid their conflict. Ask for volunteers to describe strategies that might have helped.

Closing activity
End the session with a game. You could ask for volunteers to pull a funny face to make the other children laugh. Alternatively, you could ask the children to close their eyes and relax while they listen to a few minutes of relaxing music.

> **Action plan**
>
> Use the dramas as part of a class assembly to show the work on conflict management that your group has been working on.

Extension activity

Ask the children to find examples of conflict in the books they read and to list the sequence of events until the point of falling out.

They could do the same for films or television programmes. You could make a collection of the words that are used commonly to describe conflict.

LOOKING AT SITUATIONS

This session focuses on the incidents and situations that may lead to conflict or an angry outburst.

Learning goal

I know that feelings, thoughts and behaviour are linked.

Resources

A few dictionaries, a flipchart and a pen

What to do

Opening activity

A range of statements to read to the children follow. After you read each statement, ask the children to react in a positive or negative way. For positive, they smile and clap their hands. For negative, they make an angry face and growl. Read out the situations, allowing time between them for the children to respond:

- You have been told to tidy your room.
- Someone notices that you are wearing odd socks.
- You have just been given your pocket money.
- Your best friend has gone off with someone else.
- Your teacher has given you a well-done sticker.
- You have searched everywhere but can't find your school bag.
- It is a rainy day and you have nothing to do.
- Some children won't let you join in their game.
- You are having your favourite meal tonight.
- A friend has broken your new toy.

Going deeper

Go through the list again and ask for volunteers to suggest words to describe how each situation might make someone feel; for example, irritable, embarrassed, sad, frustrated, bored, hurt, angry. Write these words on the flipchart. Ask for volunteers to look up any words new to them in a dictionary and to read out the definitions.

Divide the children into small groups. Give each group a word from the flipchart and ask each member in turn to tell the rest of their group about a situation that might make someone feel that emotion. This could be a real-life situation or a story they know or make up themselves.

Ask each group to choose a spokesperson to tell the rest of the children what their group shared.

If your children may have difficulty coping with a long list of words, you can introduce some during the preceding week. These words are very useful and even quite young children will enjoy using them. You could choose a word for the day – talk about it, tell anecdotes about when you have felt that way, point out situations when story-book characters have felt that way too.

Time to reflect

Point out that a lot of different emotions can lead to conflict. One thing they all have in common is that they make us feel uncomfortable, confused and emotionally off balance. As you are explaining this, stand on one leg. Explain that there are two things that can happen when you are off balance. You can regain your balance by concentrating on steadying yourself calmly. Illustrate this by wobbling on your standing leg and then steadying yourself. The other thing that can happen is that you fall over and risk injury – it is wise not to demonstrate this. Point out that there is a choice between these two options when conflict is involved.

Closing activity

End the session with a game called Good Thing, Bad Thing. Think of some funny situations to tell the children, such as these:

- A giant chicken followed you to school today.
- Your mum has given you your pocket money twice by mistake.
- A sudden gust of wind has blown your eyebrows off.
- A magical moonbeam has made your sweets multiply tenfold.
- Your socks have developed the cheesiest smell in the world.

After you read a statement, each child puts their thumbs up if they think it is a good thing or their thumbs down if they think it is a bad thing. It can be fun to ask some children to explain their reasoning.

Action plan

Make a display of the words and their meanings from this session. It can be a useful reference point for developing the children's emotional vocabulary.

Extension activity

Extend the idea of Good Thing, Bad Thing into story writing. You might use the situations as story starters or ask the children to invent their own situations and make them into stories.

HELPING CHILDREN DEAL WITH CONFLICT

LOOKING AT WHAT PEOPLE DO WHEN THEY FALL OUT

This session looks at angry behaviour.

Learning goal

I can recognise when I am becoming overwhelmed by my feelings.

Resources

A beanbag, a flipchart and a pen

What to do

Opening activity

Start the session with the circle game Afloat in a Boat. Use the following chant:

Thirty [or however many are in your group] *children*
Were floating in a boat.
There was a loud shout
And one fell out.

As you begin the chant, pass the beanbag to the child on your left. Continue to pass the beanbag until the chant ends. Whoever is holding the beanbag at this point must move to the centre. The chant resumes with the child on the left of the one who has moved.

Play more rounds like this, depending on how much time you have. Before the chant begins again, the child/children in the centre are allowed to guess who they think will be out this time. If they are correct, they are allowed to rejoin the circle. Don't forget to adjust the number used in the rhyme each time.

Going deeper

Write 'Storm' on the flipchart. Discuss what words this brings to mind for the children.

Record these words on the flipchart. Talk about what dangers and consequences are associated with storms. Record these on the flipchart too.

Write 'Anger' on a new page. Point out that anger can build up just like a storm. Talk about the way in which storms build up – it starts to rain, the wind gets stronger, the rain gets heavier, thunder and lightning begin and a lovely day turns awful. Sometimes you know a storm is brewing because you can hear the distant thunder, see the rain coming and the lightning, and feel stronger wind.

Talk about how we can be aware of anger rising in ourselves in the same way. Ask the children to tell you any signs that indicate that they are getting angry. They may say things like feeling hot, dizziness, feeling as if they are going to explode, feeling tearful.

Explain that when someone becomes angry their body changes. There is an increased blood flow to the muscles and the brain's reasoning skills don't function as well as they normally would. This is why people may do things when they are angry that they wouldn't do when they are calm. This means that they are more likely to get into disputes with other people.

Ask the children to describe what often happens when people fall out. They might say that people shout, sulk, cry, fight, call each other names, damage property, and so on. Make a list of their responses on the flipchart.

Play a game during which the children pretend to be calm and then angry. Ask them to walk around the room calmly. When you clap your hands, they need to stop, turn to a person near them, perform a star jump, put on an angry face and shout 'Whaaa'. Repeat this several times.

Time to reflect

Call the children back together and ask them to think about some conflicts that they have been involved in. Ask for volunteers to suggest words that describe how they felt before, during and after the incident.

Closing activity

End the session with a round using the sentence stem: 'One way that helps me to keep calm is . . .'.

> **Action plan**
>
> Many disputes are caused by poor social skills. Run a good manners incentive scheme with your group whereby they receive a suitable reward, such as choosing a game for the group to play, when they reach a certain target.

Extension activity

Give each child two sheets of paper, a pencil and some resources to colour the pictures they will produce. On one sheet ask them to draw a sad scene entitled 'Falling out' in which a dispute is taking place. Ask the children to choose colours that reflect the highly charged nature of the picture. On the second sheet, the children need to create a scene called 'Getting on' in which the scene and colours reflect this title. If they wish, they could add words that communicate the feelings of the participants in each scene.

HELPING CHILDREN DEAL WITH CONFLICT

MAKING UP IS HARD TO DO

This session focuses on the emotional impact of conflict and looks at strategies for making up.

Learning goal

I know that how I act and react has an impact on others.

Resources

A flipchart and a pen

What to do

Opening activity

Tell the children to spread out and ask them to think about how someone might look when they feel sad. They should imagine how their face might look, how they might hold their body and how they might move. Ask them to walk around in this manner. After a couple of minutes, stop them and ask them to repeat the exercise in a happy manner.

Going deeper

Form a circle and revisit the work on the damage caused by falling out with someone. Discuss how these difficulties can be obstacles to reconciliation, and so even when we know it will be better to make friends it can be very hard to do so. Spend some time thinking about what these obstacles may be, recording the children's comments on the flipchart. They may suggest such things as these:

- It's hard to say sorry.
- You want revenge.
- You feel too hurt.
- You don't know how to make up.

- You think it's the other person's fault.
- You feel embarrassed.

Tell the children that you will teach them ways of making up that will help them to settle arguments by finding them the best solution for everyone involved.

Time to reflect

Ask the children to sit in a relaxed manner with their eyes closed and their hands in their laps while they listen to you reading the following:

Let's think about what it means to be a good and trustworthy friend. A good friend is loyal and tries not to let others down. They don't talk about others behind their backs. They are thoughtful and know how to share things. Friends like these are ones that we should like to keep. When we fall out, we need to remember these things so that they can remind us to help each other to make up and be friends again.

Closing activity

End the session with a game of The Ministry of Silly Walks, asking for small groups of volunteers who wouldn't normally play outside together (although they might in the future) to agree upon a funny walk to perform to the others.

Action plan

Ask the children to contribute to a classroom Friendship Charter, in which they list the things that they look for in a friend. You can display the charter on the classroom wall as a reminder of the behaviours that you wish to encourage.

Explore the use of puppets as a means of teaching social skills. They are an excellent way to explore disputes, and provide children with a wonderful opportunity to advise others while teaching themselves. A script to use with puppets for younger children follows this session.

Extension activity

Ask the children to write letters to an imaginary agony aunt, seeking advice on how best to resolve a fictional conflict between friends. They can then take the part of the agony aunt and reply to their own or someone else's letter.

Using puppets with younger children

Puppets are a valuable teaching aid as they help children to suspend disbelief, seeing them as real characters interacting with each other. For this activity you will need to read through the script that follows in advance to give you guidance about how to present the three parts (use different voices, if your acting skills permit this). You need two animal puppets.

Ask the children to sit in a circle, put a pair of scissors in front of you and place a puppet on either hand. You will need to address the puppets as though they are members of a class. Tell the children that the puppets are going to help with a story.

HELPING CHILDREN DEAL WITH CONFLICT

Teacher: Well done, class. You've worked really hard. Now it's time to tidy up, so put all the equipment away, please.

Both puppets pick up the scissors at the same time.

Raj: I'm putting the scissors away.

Sol: No, you're not. I'm putting them away. I had them first.

Raj: No, you didn't. I had them first. Let go.

Sol: No, you let go!

The two puppets pull at the pair of scissors. Eventually Sol lets go, then pushes Raj in anger. Raj drops the scissors and begins to cry.

Teacher: My goodness me, whatever is happening? Why are you crying, Raj? What is the matter?

Raj: I was putting the scissors away and Sol tried to snatch them and pushed me over.

Sol: I had them first. He took them from me.

Teacher: I think you need to sort out this squabble. What do you think you should do?

Turn to the children and ask them to help Raj and Sol resolve their dispute. Discuss the options that the children suggest, looking at the pros and cons to find the most suitable. Act this resolution with the puppets. Comment on how thinking through issues can sometimes prevent squabbles getting out of control.

LOOKING AT ARGUMENTS

This session looks at evaluating solutions to conflicts to see if they are fair. If they are unfair, the children will be asked to work together to suggest fair outcomes.

Learning goal
I can resolve conflicts so that everyone feels positive about the outcome.

Resources
Enough copies of page 23 for one per pair/group.

What to do

Opening activity
Start the session by reading out a list of items such as popcorn, Superman, skateboards, broccoli, ice cream, teddy bears, spiders. After you read out an item, the children need to decide whether they like it or not. If they do, they answer 'Yes'; if they don't, they answer 'No'. Alternatively, they could stand for yes and remain seated for no.

Going deeper

Discuss how arguments happen all the time – children, adults and even countries fall out. Explain that it is impossible to stop all arguments, but we can learn ways to make up when we fall out with others. As people often don't know how to do this, this session will teach them how to resolve conflicts so that everyone involved is happy with the outcome. Tell the children that an important thing to remember when making up is that the solution must be fair to everyone.

Put the children into pairs or small groups and give each pair/group a copy of page 23. Try to make sure you have a good reader in each group. If not, read each scenario out in turn and allow time for the groups to consider whether each one is fair or unfair. Allow 5 minutes for this activity. Gather the groups together and ask what their findings were.

Time to reflect

Send the groups away again to consider better solutions for the scenarios they have identified as having unfair outcomes. After 5 minutes, call the children back to the circle to discuss their solutions.

If you are working with younger children, you could use the following puppet script, in which the two puppets are having an argument, as a guide to help the children explore fair solutions. The role play begins with the two puppets fighting.

Teacher: Raj and Sol, please stop this fighting at once. Now, what is going on?

Sol: Raj has got all the cars and won't let me have any.

Teacher: Raj, those cars are for everyone to play with. If Sol wants to play with them as well, what do you need to do?

Raj (grumpily): I should share them with him.

Teacher: Well done, Raj. That's right, you should share the toys.

Raj: Right, there are six cars. You can have one and I'll have five.

Ask the children if this is a fair solution. Ask them for suggestions to make the outcome fair. When they have agreed on a suitable solution, act it out with the puppets.

> **Action plan**
>
> Use drama and role play to explore scenarios with unfair consequences. Discuss alternative endings to the role plays that all participants would find acceptable. Perform the role plays again using the new endings.

Closing activity

Explain that you will begin this game by saying the word 'Zoom' to the person on your right in the circle. This word is then passed round the circle. However, if a child whose turn it is says 'Eek' instead, this reverses the direction of play and 'Zoom' must then travel in the opposite direction.

The danger with this game is that 'Eek' will be said so frequently that it will grind to a halt. This is an example of an unfair situation for some of the participants. Ask the children if they can devise a solution to this problem, such as each child is only allowed to say 'Eek' once during the course of the game. Discuss and/or try out any suggestions to see if they are viable.

Fair and unfair scenarios

Scenario 1

Jamie and Ben have been arguing about the rules of a card game. They have a chat to try to sort things out. Jamie tells Ben that if he decides on the rules and they do what he says, they won't argue any more.

Scenario 2

India wants to play with the skipping ropes but Meg wants to play a clapping game. They argue and fall out. After a while, they try to make up. Meg suggests that they could skip for 10 minutes and then clap for 10 minutes.

Scenario 3

Josh and Tariq had a fight because Josh kept the comic all wet playtime and would not let Tariq see it. Josh said that he had it first and so he could keep it as long as he wanted.

Scenario 4

Zoe and Jade have fallen out because Zoe called Jade a nasty name. Zoe says it was because Jade and Sita went off at playtime without her. Zoe says that she is sorry she called Jade a name and Jade says that she is sorry she did not include Zoe in her game with Sita. Next playtime, they will try to play together.

Scenario 5

It is playtime and one group's table is messy. There are two rubbers, twelve pencils, five rulers and several pieces of paper on it. The two monitors, Leah and Sanjit, are arguing over who should tidy it up. The teacher hears them and tells them both to help. Leah tells Sanjit that she will put the rubbers away and he can tidy the rest.

HELPING CHILDREN DEAL WITH CONFLICT

AGGRESSIVE, PASSIVE AND ASSERTIVE

In this session the children investigate appropriate ways to act when seeking a successful outcome to a dispute.

Learning goal

I know the most appropriate way to act when looking for a suitable resolution to an argument.

Resources

Enough copies of page 26 for one per pair/group.

What to do

Opening activity

Ask the children to stand in a circle. Choose a child (child A) to start the game. Everyone claps their hands twice and then child A says the name of someone in the circle (child B). Child A sits down. The group claps twice again before child B names another child (child C). Child B then sits down. This process is repeated until all the children have been named and are seated. The last child standing is named by everyone.

Going deeper

Remind the children that in the last session they looked at fair outcomes to arguments. Discuss why is it important that the outcome of an argument is fair for everyone involved. Establish that if an outcome produces a win–win situation, everyone is likely to be happy and the resolution has the best chance of lasting. If someone is not happy with an outcome, the argument is likely to flare up again.

Read the conversations on page 26 to the children. If you have a teaching assistant available, they could take one of the roles. Ask the children how each child behaved. This should help them to see that there is a child acting aggressively and a child acting passively in each conversation. Explore how the outcome in each case was affected by the imbalance of power.

Time to reflect

Put the children into pairs or groups and ask them to talk through the conversations, thinking about what the children could have said and how they could have found a solution that they were both happy with. After 10 minutes or so, call the children back into a circle and discuss their findings. Choose one or two willing groups to act out their revised conversations.

Closing activity

Ask the children if, based on what they have just done, they can think of a better way of talking to someone when they want to sort out an argument. Explore the idea that each child could state their own thoughts and feelings in a calm way. This might prevent them from becoming angry or withdrawing. For older children, you might want to introduce the terms **aggressive**, **passive** and **assertive**. Point out that in the revised conversations the characters were not afraid to express themselves, but this was not at the expense of the other person.

HELPING CHILDREN DEAL WITH CONFLICT

Action plan

Once you have established the meaning of the words **passive**, **aggressive** and **assertive**, try to reinforce them by using them frequently with your children. This might be to praise positive behaviour or comment on the behaviour of others in stories.

Extension activity

Explore aggressive and passive behaviour in animals. This could be by sharing anecdotal evidence; observing and recording the behaviour of pets; or carrying out research using books, television programmes or the Internet.

How will I tell if my stick insect is being passive or aggressive?

Aggressive and passive conversations

Jermaine and Rashad are trying to sort out who plays what position in a football match.

Jermaine: Well, you can go in goal because you're not very fast. OK?

Rashad: I sort of wanted to play in defence.

Jermaine: No, you wouldn't be any good there. You should be in goal.

Rashad: Well, I thought we could choose what position we wanted to play. I've already been in goal three times this week. It's someone else's turn.

Jermaine: Yeah, but I don't want you to play in defence. I want you in goal.

Rashad: I don't really like going in goal.

Jermaine: If you want to play, you'll have to be in goal.

Rashad: (reluctantly) Oh, all right then, if I have to.

Jermaine: Good, that's settled then. We can tell Miss we've sorted things out.

Jo and Sasha are trying to sort out an argument over some work they are doing together.

Jo: You said that I could do the next drawing.

Sasha: Yeah, but I don't like doing the writing.

Jo: Well, I've done all the writing so far and I haven't done any drawings.

Sasha: You want to be my partner, don't you?

Jo: Yes.

Sasha: OK, then you have to do the writing or I won't work with you.

Jo: Couldn't I just do one of the drawings?

Sasha: No, I like drawing. You're lucky anyway, 'cos Janine wanted to be my partner and I told her I was going to work with you.

Jo: Oh, OK, but I would really like to do a drawing.

Sasha: Well you can't. You do the writing and I'll do the drawing.

© *Helping Children Deal with Conflict* LDA — Permission to Photocopy

THE SKILLS OF NEGOTIATION

This session provides an opportunity for children to learn and practise negotiation skills. Working as a group, they investigate which approaches are effective in resolving disputes.

Learning goal

I can understand another person's point of view and how they might be feeling.

Resources

Enough copies of page 28 for one per group.

What to do

Opening activity

Start the session with a game of Hunt the Toy. This works in the same way as Hunt the Thimble. One child is sent from the room while another child hides a small toy. The first child is invited back in to find the toy. They try to judge how near they are to the toy by the comments made by the other children, who use words such as **warm**, **cold**, **hot**, **scorching**. Alternatively, the children can clap quietly if the child is far from the toy and with increasing volume as they get nearer to it. Play this several times.

Going deeper

Put the children into groups of four and give each group a copy of page 28. Tell the children that they are going to look at each scenario in turn, rotating the roles between them. Two children are involved in the role play, and the other two children are observers.

Ask the children who are in role to use what they have learnt about negotiation to try to find fair solutions that provide win–win outcomes. After each role play, the observers can offer the actors constructive feedback on what they saw and anything that they might try in subsequent role plays to develop their skills.

Time to reflect

Call the children together and ask them what they found helpful about watching other people try to sort out a quarrel. It might be useful to explore the suggestions that were made to help improve negotiation skills.

Closing activity

End the session with a game of outrageous excuses to stimulate creative thinking. Pass the following sentence stem round the circle: 'The reason I haven't got my homework is because . . .'. Each child completes the sentence with a bizarre excuse, such as: an alien snatched it, a fire-breathing dragon burnt it, my pen had magic ink in it that disappeared as soon as I had finished the writing.

> **Action plan**
>
> Try to find opportunities during class time for children to practise their conflict resolution skills by exploring how they might solve fictional and real-life disputes so that they can continue to learn the language of negotiation.

Extension activity

Negotiation skills are used in a wide variety of situations. Use your current areas of study to devise relevant situations in which the children can role play negotiation techniques. For instance, RE and PSHE lessons offer opportunities to explore ethical issues related to fairness.

Quarrels

One of you needs to be child A, one child B, and the other two are observers. Choose one of the scenarios below and make up a scene in which you act out a good ending to the argument for both of you.

1. Your teacher has asked you to write a story or poem together. You can't agree on which to write.

Child A: I want to write a poem.

Child B: I want to write a story.

2. You are arguing about who had the original idea for a design that you both want to use in art.

Child A: You've copied me.

Child B: No, you copied me.

3. You have been fighting each other and are now arguing over who started it.

Child A: You pushed me first.

Child B: No, you kicked me first.

4. Two children are having a quarrel about their friendship.

Child A: You don't like me any more, do you?

Child B: I just wanted to play with someone else today.

5. Both of you are claiming you own the same small item.

Child A: That's my card.

Child B: No, it isn't, it's mine.

LOOKING AT WRONG ASSUMPTIONS

This session looks at the impact of making wrong assumptions. Children are encouraged to find out the facts behind people's actions rather than coming to their own conclusions, which may be wrong.

Learning goal

I can make a wise choice about work or behaviour.

Resources

None

What to do

Opening activity

Begin the session by miming an activity such as hanging out washing on a line. Ask volunteers to guess what you are doing. Allow some of the children to mime activities for the others to guess. After some of the guesses have proved incorrect, make a point of this. You can then comment that this sometimes happens in life too. We see people doing things and we think we know why they are acting in that way, but we are not always right.

Going deeper

Explain to the children that you are going to read them two different views of the same incident. Ask them to listen carefully as you will be asking some questions afterwards.

Danesh's view

I don't like Marc any more. He said that he would play with me yesterday and then I saw him going off with Sanjit. I called out to him and he looked at me but didn't stop. I went to the library to read a book but I felt miserable. When I saw Marc at the end of lunchtime I asked him what he was doing with Sanjit but he wouldn't tell me. I think they've been talking about me. We usually walk home together after school, but he didn't wait for me. I tried to ring him, but his mum said he was out. I don't believe her. I think Marc told her he doesn't want to talk to me. I asked for him to ring me when he got home but he didn't bother. I don't think he wants to be my friend any more. At school this morning, I didn't look at him on purpose and asked Joe to play with me. I'll show Marc that I don't need him.

Marc's view

I think Danesh is mean. I'm never going to talk to him again. Yesterday Sanjit was upset because his dog was ill and had to go to the vet. I tried to be kind and talk to him to cheer him up. He asked me to keep quiet about his dog as he thought he would cry if anyone said anything. I looked for Danesh later, but I couldn't find him. When we were lining up, he asked me what I was doing with Sanjit but I couldn't tell him. My dad fetched me to go to the dentist after school and I had forgotten to tell Danesh earlier that I couldn't walk home with him. This morning, my mum told me that Danesh had phoned last night and wanted me to ring him back, but she had forgotten to tell me. I tried to ring him then, but he had already left for school. I thought I could talk to him later, but he won't even look at me. Well, if he wants to act like that when it's not my fault, that's his problem.

A series of questions to ask the children follow. They will help them to explore what they have just heard.

> - Danesh thought that Marc and Sanjit were talking about him. Was he right?
> - When Danesh asked Marc why he had gone off with Sanjit, could Marc have said something that might have helped the situation without upsetting Sanjit?
> - Might Danesh have tried to persuade Marc to tell him what Sanjit had said? If so, what might have happened?
> - How might Marc have reacted differently when Danesh called out to him in the playground?
> - What might Danesh have thought that Marc did after school instead of walking home with him?
> - Why do you think Danesh thought that Marc hadn't rung him back? Was he right?

If you are working with younger children, you may prefer to use the puppet script that follows for this session.

Teacher: Raj, you're looking very sad. What's the matter?

Raj: Sol and I had a quarrel and now we're not friends any more.

Teacher: Oh dear, that is a shame! Wouldn't you like to be friends again?

Raj: Yes, I would, but I don't know how to make up.

Teacher: What do you think you might do?

Raj: I could try to talk to Sol, but he might not want to talk to me.

Teacher: Well, why don't you give it a try?

Raj: Sol, will you talk to me?

Sol: Hmm, I don't know. I am cross with you.

Raj: I'm sad that we're not friends any more. I want to be friends again.

Sol: Yes, but you called me a nasty name.

Raj: I'm very sorry if I hurt your feelings. I got carried away. Please can we be friends again?

Sol: OK. Let's go and do something fun.

Teacher (to children): Do you think that Raj did the right thing? What else could you do to make up? What else might you say to someone you've argued with to try to make things right?

Time to reflect

Ask the children to explain how the two characters are feeling and what they think might happen next. Look at the potential positive and negative outcomes. Point out that both characters made assumptions and misinterpreted the other's actions. Explain that everyone can make incorrect assumptions about how others feel because we misinterpret their actions. In a dispute it is important to find out the facts rather than jumping to conclusions that are usually wrong.

Closing activity

End the session with a round using the following sentence starter: 'An important thing that I have learned in this session is . . .'.

HELPING CHILDREN DEAL WITH CONFLICT

Action plan

Use the scripts for Marc and Danesh in a presentation to another group or in an assembly to show others what your group has been learning. This will be a real boost to your group's confidence and identity.

Extension activity

Finish with this light-hearted game. Give each child a piece of paper and a pencil. Ask them to complete the sentence 'He said ...' at the top of the sheet. For example, 'He said "I just saw a pink elephant."' They then fold the paper so that what they wrote cannot be seen and pass it on to the child on their left. This child then completes the sentence 'She said ...' further down the page. For example, 'She said, "I like dancing too."' They fold the paper and pass it on. The third child writes where this conversation took place before folding it and passing it on. The fourth child writes what happened next; for example, 'They had pizza for tea.' The next child then unfolds the sheet of paper passed to them. In turn, they read out the sequence.

THE PEACE PROCESS

Building on the work the children have done on negotiation skills, this session focuses on what other factors might help to make a solution to a dispute successful.

Learning goal

I can solve problems by reviewing the possible solutions, identifying their advantages and disadvantages, implementing a solution and subsequently evaluating its success.

Resources

A flipchart and a pen

What to do

Opening activity

Begin the session with a circle game. Turn to the child on your right and smile at them broadly. They turn to the person on their right and repeat this action. The smile is passed round the circle in this manner. As you become more proficient, try to send the smile round as quickly as possible. You can start the game with a child or have two smiles starting at different points round the circle.

Going deeper

Remind the children that they have been exploring quarrels and how to solve them peacefully. Explain that you want to create an area in the room where they could go if they need to make up with someone. Ask the children for their suggestions about how to make the area suitable for this activity. You could record their ideas on the flipchart. If you need to prompt them, you could suggest that it should be a quiet area that offers a bit of privacy, with a small table and a couple of chairs.

Time to reflect

Having established the basic position and layout of your quiet corner, ask the children what else they would like to have there to help and encourage people towards a peaceful solution. Paper and pencils might be helpful, as might a sign to indicate that negotiations are in progress. You could include symbols that represent peace and calm, such as a dove, a calm seascape and a rainbow. You could print suitable images from the Internet or ask the children to produce their own. You could include slogans to remind children what they are at the peace table for, such as 'Don't break friends, make friends'.

Closing activity

End the session with an enjoyable game. Put the children in pairs. One child in each pair has a minute to make their partner laugh. They can do this in any way that they like, such as pulling funny faces and telling jokes, but they can't touch their partner. After a minute, swap roles.

> **Action plan**
>
> Make sure that you use rewards to praise those children who don't get into disputes. This is especially important when you first set up your peace area as initially every child will want to use it.

Extension activity

It is a good idea to place copies of a peace process chart near your peace area. The photocopiable resource on page 33 provides a format for the children to use, giving them suitable language to use and a clear process to work through to reach an appropriate solution.

Talk the children through the chart and review how it is being used in the first few weeks.

Let's make up

We fell out over ....
....
....
....

1. I did ....
....
....
....

2. I did ....
....
....
....

What would we like to happen? ....
....
....
....

How will we make this happen? ....
....
....
....

USING 'I' STATEMENTS

This session aims to show that the language you use can have an important impact on the outcome of negotiations. The children will use role play as that often gives participants a better understanding of a situation than simply talking about it.

Learning goal

I understand that the way I express my feelings can change the way other people feel.

Resources

A lightweight ball

What to do

Opening activity

Ask the children to stand in a circle. Give one child the ball. This child thinks of a positive adjective to describe the group. They say their word, and then bounce or roll the ball to another child before sitting down. This continues until everyone has said their word. The final child bounces or rolls the ball to you.

Going deeper

Comment on the positive nature of the game that you have been playing. Hearing the sorts of words that were used helps us to feel good about ourselves. However, when we accuse someone of something, that can have the opposite effect, making them feel upset, angry, guilty, defensive or a combination of these.

Explain that they are going to learn a way to tell someone that they are upset which reduces the risk of making the situation worse or of provoking the person. Say the following two sentences to the children:

- 'You upset me when you swore at me.'
- 'I felt upset when you swore at me.'

Ask the children what differences they noticed in the words you used. Someone is likely to mention the use of 'I' in the second sentence. Explain that by doing this and saying how you feel, such statements are perceived as assertive rather than aggressive. They indicate that you are taking responsibility for how you are feeling. They also ensure that the issue of blame is set aside. The message has still been delivered, but in a way that will contribute towards the process of making up and finding an appropriate solution.

Give the children the following examples to change into 'I' statements. They need to think carefully about the emotion that they want to address in each case. Discuss their suggestions.

- You made me drop the pencils when you pushed me.
- You made me angry when you went off with Joe.
- You hurt me when you kicked me.

Ask the children to think about the following incidents and make an 'I' statement for each in turn. Explore their findings.

- You have told a friend a secret and they told someone else.
- Someone took your snack and threw it on the floor.
- A child has said that they don't want to sit by you.

Time to reflect

Sometimes it is helpful to extend an 'I' statement as follows:

> • 'I felt upset when you swore at me because you used a hurtful word. What I would like is for you to try not to do that when you feel cross.'

Such a statement addresses how you feel, what happened to contribute to your feeling like that, why it was upsetting, and what you would like to happen in the future. You could take some of the examples from the previous two lists and ask the children to extend the 'I' statements they had previously devised.

You might find it helpful to have a reminder of this formula on the wall near your peace area.

Action plan

Make sure that you model the use of 'I' statements when working with your children.

Closing activity

End the session with a round using the sentence stem 'One good thing that happened to me this week is . . .'.

Extension activity

Put the children in pairs and give them a sheet of paper and a pencil. Ask one child in each pair to write up to five 'you' statements. Their partner can help them if necessary. They then give the sheet to their partner, who tries to reframe them as 'I' statements. Ask for volunteers to share one or two examples.

LOOKING AT THE IMPORTANCE OF LISTENING

This session shows that listening well is an important aspect of negotiation and conflict resolution.

Learning goal

I can understand another person's point of view and how they might be feeling.

Resources

Two photocopies of page 37.

What to do

Opening activity

Ask the children to sit in a circle. Start the session with a game of Chinese Whispers. Choose a suitable sentence to send round the circle, such as 'Polar bears live in the Arctic Circle but penguins live in the Antarctic.' Stress that each child must whisper the message and say it once only. If someone is unsure of what was said to them they must pass on what they think they heard. It's always very amusing to hear what the sentence is like when the round comes to an end.

Going deeper

Recap on what you have learnt so far on how to develop an effective peace process. Tell the children that in this session they will be looking at one of the most important aspects of this process.

Choose two confident readers to stand in the centre of the circle, facing each other. Give each child a photocopy of page 37, folded to show one paragraph and questions only. Ask one child to read paragraph A to themselves and the other child to read paragraph B. When they are ready, count to 3 and then both children should read their paragraph aloud at the same time. They must try to concentrate on what they are saying and not stop reading until they have come to the end.

Beneath each paragraph are a series of questions. When the children have finished reading their texts, tell them to take turns to ask each other the questions related to their section. You could open these to the group too. It should become clear that there are very few, if any, questions that can be accurately answered. Discuss how both children talking simultaneously meant that it was difficult to listen properly to what each other was saying.

Time to reflect

Tell the children that actively listening to what the other person is saying is a very important part of making up. Sometimes when two people are arguing, they are both trying to have their say at the same time or concentrating on what they want to say next. They don't listen properly to what the other person is saying. If you don't try to listen carefully and fairly to each other, the dispute will get worse and the chance of finding a fair solution will decrease.

Closing activity

End the session with a game of Simon Says. This is great fun and excellent for listening skills.

> **Action plan**
>
> Good-quality listening skills are valuable in many aspects of your work with children. Think about whether you consider how to utilise and teach listening skills in other curriculum areas.

Extension activity

Improve the children's listening skills by dividing your group into pairs and giving them a minute each to find out three to five facts about their partner to tell the rest of the class. You can vary the time and number of facts depending on the age of your group. Alternatively, you could read out a list of connected items – such as five types of trees, rivers or capital cities – and ask the children to try to repeat them back afterwards. You can make this more challenging by giving the list before playtime and asking them to recall it afterwards. You can discuss what strategies they used as they listened in order to process and store the information.

Listening skills

Paragraph A

Five children went to play in the park. There were three girls and two boys. The park was down the street, so they went there after breakfast. They played on the slide and swings. It was good fun and everyone enjoyed themselves. Later it was time to go home. One of the girls realised that she had lost her red hat. She was upset because her granny made it and gave it to her for her birthday. They hunted high and low for it and found it, at last, on the climbing frame. It was lunchtime when they left the park.

Questions

1. How many boys were there?
2. Where was the park?
3. When did they set off for the park?
4. What was lost?
5. What time did they leave the park?

Paragraph B

Two friends went to the seaside. Their names were Ahmed and Zak. They built a huge sandcastle on the beach with four towers and windows made of shells. Ahmed used his sock on a stick for a flag. It was a lovely warm day and the boys splashed in the sea. Zak even went for a swim. Afterwards, they ate some sandwiches they had brought with them. Zak had cheese sandwiches, which were his favourite. Ahmed found a crab in a rock pool when he was paddling. He quickly jumped out as he didn't want it to nip his toes.

Questions

1. How many towers did the sandcastle have?
2. What did Ahmed use for a flag?
3. Who swam in the sea?
4. What did Zak have in his sandwiches?
5. What did Ahmed see in the rock pool?

© Helping Children Deal with Conflict LDA   Permission to Photocopy

HELPING AND HINDERING THE PEACE PROCESS

This session aims to help the children to understand other factors that can help or hinder them in their attempts to resolve conflicts.

Learning goal

I can express a range of feelings in ways that don't hurt others or myself.

Resources

A large sheet of paper and a pen, and a quoit or beanbag for each child

What to do

Opening activity

Give each child a beanbag or quoit to place on their head. They then walk around while trying to keep it in place. If it falls off, they must stop moving and wait for someone to pick it up and hand it back to them. If the rescuer drops their own beanbag or quoit in their attempt to pick up a fallen one, they must stand still too.

Going deeper

Remind the children that they have been looking at ways of making up when they fall out. In this session they are going to look at what things can help to reach a resolution and what things might make it harder. Fold the sheet of paper in half horizontally. Write 'Things that help making up' as the title for the top half and 'Things that hinder making up' in the bottom half. Ask the children to suggest some ideas for the bottom section.

Some examples are:

- feeling angry;
- shouting;
- swearing;
- name calling;
- accusations;
- angry gestures;
- interrupting;
- not listening;
- making unreasonable demands;
- invading another's body space;
- being unwilling to make up.

When the children have run out of suggestions, ask them to think of helpful things for the top half of the sheet. Some suggestions are:

- willingness to set aside differences;
- actively listening to the other person;
- using respectful language;
- not making assumptions;
- stating calmly why you are cross and what you would like to happen;
- admitting if you have done something wrong;
- saying sorry;
- asking the other person what they would like to happen;
- taking turns to speak and listen;
- considering the other person's point of view.

Time to reflect

When you have completed this, you could ask the children to work out a list of helpful hints that could be displayed in your peace area.

Closing activity

Choose five animals with distinctive calls, such as a cow, a sheep, a cat, a dog, and a cuckoo. Ask the children to practise each of the calls in turn. Tell them to spread out and quietly tell each child which animal they are. On your word the children move about, making the sound of the animal you gave them. As they find members of their group, they stay together. When they think their group is complete, they sit down.

Extension activity

It is a good idea to record the positive resolutions that your children find for their conflicts. These can be displayed in the peace area.

These are examples:

- I asked her to play with me next playtime and we decided together on the game we would play.
- I said that I was sorry for upsetting him and we both said 'Make friends, make friends, never, never break friends.'
- We counted to 10 together and then we smiled at each other and started again.
- We shook hands and realised it was a silly argument.
- We decided that we would ask someone else to watch us play cards and they would be the referee.
- I said that I would try not to provoke him and he said he would try not to lose his temper.

USING THE CREATIVE ARTS TO EXPLORE CONFLICT RESOLUTION

Using creative arts, such as poetry writing and drawing, can help children reflect on the impact of conflict on themselves and others.

Learning goal

I can choose my words carefully in disputes.

Resources

A lightweight ball, paper, pencils and art materials

What to do

Opening activity

Ask the children to stand in a circle and practise throwing or bouncing the ball from child to child. Use the theme of 'A happy group is . . .'. Ask each child to think of a word to describe a happy class. As each child receives the ball they say their word, before passing the ball on. It doesn't matter if the same word is used a number of times.

Going deeper

Read the following poem to the children.

Daniel was my friend

Daniel was my friend, once upon a time.

I played at his house and he played at mine.

Like two peas in a pod, we were always together.

Everyone said we were birds of a feather.

We laughed and we joked, and we promised to share.

When I needed him, he always was there.

One day something happened and it wasn't the same,

I hid from the trouble and I didn't share the blame.

And when he tried to talk to me so we could sort it out,

I said it was his fault and he could take the clout.

Daniel was upset and his face was full of worry,

But I didn't tell him, like I should, that I was really sorry.

I wish I'd had the courage to own up to the crime,

Daniel was a friend of mine, once upon a time.

Ask the children what they think took place. You might discuss what happened between the two children, as well as what may have caused the dispute.

You could talk about what the narrator could have done to try to save the friendship. How do they think the narrator felt about the outcome of the dispute?

Time to reflect

Ask the children to think of an alternative ending for the poem. They could suggest ideas or go away and try and rewrite the last three lines. An alternative ending that you might want to use follows:

*I plucked up my courage and said I was sorry.
I admitted I had taken part and so, in the end,
I took the punishment but kept my friend.*

> **Action plan**
>
> Collate the words from the opening activity and make them into a poster to display in your room.

Closing activity

Close the session with a circle game. Turn to the child on your right and greet them with a small bow. They turn to the person on their right and repeat this action. The bow is passed round the circle in this way. Try other greetings, such as a high five or a handshake.

Extension activity

Ask the children to produce a two-part poem for a wall display about falling out and making up. The first part of the poem on falling out could be written on a black background to represent the gloomy feelings. It could be decorated with fiery tongues to represent anger. The second part of the poem, to do with making up, could use calmer colours, such as greens and blues. This could be an individual or paired activity.

HELPING CHILDREN WHO ARE UNABLE TO RESOLVE CONFLICTS

This section is designed to give you ideas for what to do with children who find it very difficult to sort out disputes. There is likely to be a small number of children who will struggle to use the skills and processes necessary to resolve their conflicts satisfactorily. Their own emotional turmoil may prevent them from benefiting from the work that you have been doing with their group. There are a number of ways in which you can try to work with such children.

Small-group work

This approach can provide valuable help for those children with poor social skills, giving them the opportunity to learn and practise important skills in a relaxed atmosphere.

When children are frequently involved in disputes and have problems resolving them, you will often find that they lack basic social skills, such as turn taking, listening to others without interruption, sharing, politeness and empathy. All of these skills are vital for forming positive relationships. A small group consisting of an adult, the child, a friend or friends and one or two role models is an ideal way to develop these skills. A small-group session should follow a carefully planned timetable of activities such as follows, which promote speaking and listening and other interpersonal skills.

Greeting

The children sit in a circle. One child throws a beanbag to another child, saying a greeting, such as 'Hello, [name]', as they do so.

Circle activity

The children play a game called Fruit Basket. Choose two or three fruits, depending on the size of your group, and assign one to each child in the circle. When you say a fruit, the children in that category swap seats. When you say 'Fruit basket', all the children exchange places. If you have only a few children in the group, call two fruits each time.

Circle activity

Put the children into pairs and ask them to take turns to mirror their partner's actions. Tell the child thinking of the actions to move slowly and deliberately to make it easy for their partner to keep up with them.

Co-operative task

The children complete a co-operative task, such as making sandwiches or cutting up and reassembling photos from magazines to create humorous characters.

Drink and biscuits

Having a time to sit down together and share refreshments provides a valuable opportunity to chat with the children. This is an excellent time to focus on turn taking and good manners. The children work in pairs to set a table with plates, cups, drinks and biscuits. One child hands out the biscuits while the other pours the drinks. Afterwards they clear away and wash and wipe up.

Ending ritual

The children sit together for a story, clapping rhyme or song, and finish by saying goodbye to each other.

Even very challenging children respond well to this type of timetable. Away from the pressures and expectations of the larger group, they can interact with adults and other children in a less formal and more relaxed way. Moreover, since the focus is on interpersonal rather than academic skills, they can become successful regardless of intellectual ability.

Some children will have very limited opportunities for conversation at home and so a small group, with its emphasis on speaking and listening, can provide them with additional time in which to practise these skills.

Using mediation to help resolve conflict

Using other children to help resolve conflicts can sometimes have a greater impact than advice proffered by adults. If you find that some children are experiencing problems arriving at a satisfactory outcome, peer mediation may provide the answer.

There are various forms of peer mediation, all of which work best when members of staff and lunchtime supervisors have had some in-service training to understand the process involved.

Peer mediation is not a suitable intervention for disputes such as those that involve violence or a major infringement of school rules – these should be dealt with by an appropriate member of staff.

The children selected to act as mediators should undergo some training and be able to:

- help the children involved in a dispute to decide what is the best outcome for all involved;
- listen effectively to the problems, needs and feelings of the children involved;
- report back what they have been told to another person;
- act in a friendly and impartial manner;
- be non-judgemental – it is not their role to tell other children off.

You will need to establish an area where mediation takes place, and a system by which children bring their concerns to a mediator. Lunchtime often provides a good opportunity to operate the scheme as this allows sufficient time for the procedures to be followed through. Any disputes that are not settled can be rescheduled to another day or passed on to a member of staff.

The mediators should meet regularly with a member of staff to talk through any issues so that they are provided with support and encouragement. They can use their initial meeting to formulate a list of questions to ask and a routine to follow during mediation sessions.

HELPING CHILDREN DEAL WITH CONFLICT

General advice for helping children who are unable to resolve conflicts

These children often lack empathy and don't appreciate other people's feelings. Their lack of engagement means that they can dismiss the feelings of others. You may find it helpful to appeal to these children on a cognitive level of fair/unfair.

It might help some children to think about the benefits that are gained from getting on with others. By focusing on the things that they like and enjoy, you can explore positive emotions such as happiness, contentment, excitement and pride, and contrast these with the negative feelings aroused by conflict.

Enhancing their self-esteem can help some children who get into conflicts because of a deficit in this area. Finding the things they are good at and encouraging their classmates to praise them will help them to appreciate their own talents and worth. You can also look for opportunities to praise and boost them in the classroom, being particularly careful that you are not giving out unhelpful or negative messages.

Keep a diary of children's conflicts detailing the time, the cause and the other person involved to see if a pattern emerges.

If a child refuses to try to resolve a conflict, look for an inducement rather than a punishment as a spur to co-operation. Since resolving conflict is a measure of responsibility, you might offer the child a responsibility of their choice if they are willing to participate in negotiations.

Changing a pattern of behaviour is difficult. If you can encourage children to take small incremental steps in the right direction, you will be helping them towards a more positive future.

Keeping yourself on track

Your attitude can play an important part in helping children towards a peaceful resolution to a dispute. Don't underestimate the valuable input you can give. Your attitude can greatly enhance the success of the resolving-conflict programme. You should maintain a positive focus over time and avoid certain pitfalls. The following advice should help you:

- Though there is a need to regulate the length of time that children spend in the peace area, don't put undue pressure on them to finish or you will undermine the process and curb their emerging capabilities to resolve their conflicts by themselves.

- If you talk to the children about their actions in a dispute, keep your comments impersonal and focus on the action and not the child. If you give children negative labels they will live up to them.

- Be aware of the differences between disputes and incidents of bullying. The latter involve a deliberate, repeated action, which is done with the intention of hurting someone and involves an imbalance of power.

- Check that your reading of a situation is correct and don't make assumptions based on past experience. Just because a child has done something in the past, it doesn't mean that they have repeated the behaviour.

- Make sure that you treat all children fairly and that your attitude towards each child is the same.

- Model the language of the peace process for the children to experience and learn from – make sure that your own disputes with children are examples of good practice. This is by far the best way to teach others.

- Show the children that you have faith in their capabilities to resolve their own conflicts. Your belief in their ability to find a successful outcome is more likely to empower them to succeed.

Now that you have reached the end of the programme, your children should understand the causes and mechanics of disputes, and be equipped with the knowledge and experience to resolve them peacefully by themselves. There is a photocopiable list on page 46 to help you to review your practice, highlight areas of development and continue the good work that you have started.

Maintaining an effective peace process

Answer the questions in the checklist below to see whether you are maintaining a positive influence on the peace process in your classroom.

1. Is your language about the peace process still positive and affirming?

2. Do you check from time to time that the process has maintained its vigour and effectiveness?

3. Are you remembering to adopt the same unbiased attitude to all the children in your class?

4. Do you still congratulate those children who have resolved their disputes peacefully?

5. Do you check up on any children who are using the peace area frequently to ascertain the reasons behind this?

6. Do you maintain a positive focus in your class with a praise, rather than a blame, ethos?

7. Do you actively encourage tolerance and friendliness in your group?

8. Do you incorporate team-building activities into your timetable to help promote positive group dynamics?

RESOURCES

Mosley, J. (1993) *Turn your School Round*
Mosley, J. (1996) *Quality Circle Time*
Mosley, J. (1998) *More Quality Circle Time*
Mosley, J. (2006) *Using Rewards Wisely*
Mosley, J. and Sonnet, H. (2002) *101 Games for Self-Esteem*
Mosley, J. and Sonnet, H. (2002) *Making Waves*
Mosley, J. and Sonnet, H. (2003) *101 Games for Social Skills*
Mosley, J. and Sonnet, H. (2005) *Better Behaviour through Golden Time*
Mosley, J. and Sonnet, H. (2006) *101 Games for Better Behaviour*
Mosley, J. and Sonnet, H. (2006) *Helping Children Deal with Bullying*
Mosley, J. and Sonnet, H. (2006) *Helping Children Deal with Anger*
Mosley, J. and Thorp, G. (2005) *Positive Playtimes*

Mosley, J. (2000) *Quality Circle Time in Action*
Mosley, J. (2000) *Quality Circle Time Kit*
Mosley, J. (2004) *Reward Certificates*
Mosley, J. (2004) *Stickers*
Mosley, J. (2005) *Golden Rules Poster*
Mosley, J. and Sonnet, H. (2005) *Lunchtimes Poster Set*
Mosley, J. and Sonnet, H. (2005) *Playground Poster Set*
Mosley, J. (2005) *Playground Stars*

All these resources are published in Cambridge by LDA. For information about the full range of Jenny Mosley's books and resources, please contact LDA Customer Services on 0845 120 4776 or visit our website at www.LDAlearning.com

Training in the Quality Circle Time model

For information about training, contact Jenny Mosley Consultancies:

Telephone: 01225 767157

E-mail: circletime@jennymosley.co.uk

Website: www.circle-time.co.uk

Address: 28a Gloucester Road, Trowbridge, Wiltshire, BA14 0AA